Painting a Peaceful Picture

• Respecting Peers •

By T. M. Merk

The Child's World®
childsworld.com

Published by The Child's World®
1980 Lookout Drive • Mankato, MN 56003-1705
800-599-READ • www.childsworld.com

Photographs: Pressmaster/Shutterstock.com, cover, 1, 5,
9, 11, 14; Kiryl Padabed/Shutterstock.com, 7; HYS_NP/
Shutterstock.com, 13; Rawpixel.com/Shutterstock.com, 17;
Leif Eliasson/Shutterstock.com, 19
Icons: © Aridha Prassetya/Dreamstime, 3, 5, 6, 11, 12,
14, 17, 22

ISBN HARDCOVER: 9781503827462
ISBN PAPERBACK: 9781622434435
LCCN: 2017961938

Printed in the United States of America
PA02379

About the Author

T.M. Merk is an elementary educator
with a master's degree in elementary
education from Lesley University in
Cambridge, Massachusetts. Drawing
on years of classroom experience, she
enjoys creating engaging educational
material that inspires students' passion
for learning. She lives in New Hampshire
with her husband and her dog, Finn.

Table of Contents

Painting a Peaceful Picture 4

Respectful Talk 20

S.T.E.A.M. Activity 21

Glossary 22

To Learn More 23

Index 24

Painting a Peaceful Picture

Ella, Cal, and Molly wanted to paint a picture to hang in the school. They tried to plan it, but they could not agree!

"Let's paint a rainbow!" said Ella.

"No, a tree," argued Cal.

Have you ever worked in a group with someone who tried to take over the project? This can make other people in the group feel unimportant and sad. Be sure to share your ideas without making other people feel like they don't get to participate. Be a leader but not a boss.

Everyone talked over each other. No one could hear anyone else.

Then a voice cried, "Excuse me!"

Is it possible to disagree respectfully? Yes! Use the sentence starters at the end of this book to help. Working in groups can be difficult because people might have strong opinions about their ideas. The key is to be a good listener and give everyone a turn to share ideas.

Leo the paintbrush waved to the students.

"You're all good artists," he said, "and you all have great ideas. Why are you fighting?"

"We can't agree," said Molly.

"It's time to brush up on respect," Leo said. "I heard each of you give good ideas. Have any of you listened to someone else's ideas?"

"No," said Cal. "I don't think any of us listened to anyone else."

"When you work together, it's **respectful** to listen to everyone's ideas. Then you can find a fair way to agree," Leo said.

Have you ever thought to yourself, "That isn't fair!" Do you know what "fair" really means? "Fair" means that everyone gets what he or she needs. It does not mean that everyone gets the same thing. It also does not mean that someone wins and someone loses. Something is fair as long as everyone can share ideas and listen respectfully. You might even change your mind when you hear another person's great idea!

"How can it be fair if one idea wins?" asked Molly.

"Working together is about **cooperation**," Leo said. "It's not about winning and losing. It's your job to make an **agreement** as a team."

Have you ever heard the phrase "There's no *I* in *team*"? It means that a team cannot work well unless it is united. You will probably work on many teams in your life. You may be part of a team for a sport, a game, or even your job when you grow up! Knowing how to be a good sport and a great team player is an important life skill!

T together
E everyone
A achieves
M more

13

! Compromise is a big part of working in a group. When you compromise, you can use everyone's ideas, at least a little. Making sure that everyone in your group participates is another way to make everyone feel important and respected.

"We should find out why each idea is good," said Ella. "We can take turns telling the group about our idea."

Cal jumped up. "What if we painted everyone's ideas? That would be a truly **peaceful** picture!"

"I get it!" said Molly. "Respecting your **peers** creates peace. So if we all **contribute**, the picture that we make will be peaceful!"

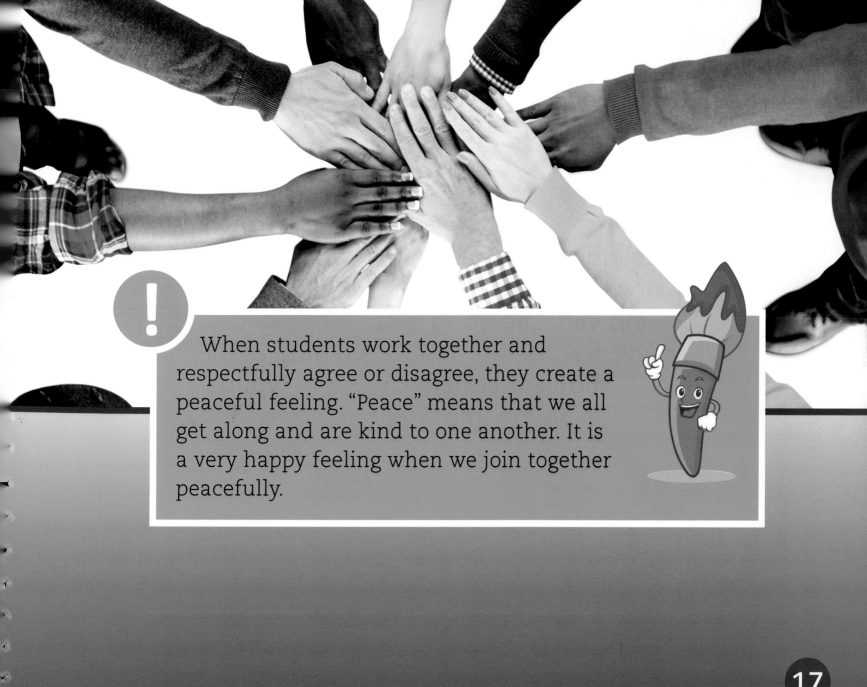

When students work together and respectfully agree or disagree, they create a peaceful feeling. "Peace" means that we all get along and are kind to one another. It is a very happy feeling when we join together peacefully.

The students got to work. They were proud of the picture that they painted together.

Respectful Talk

Do you need help talking in a respectful way about your peers?
Do you want to learn how to disagree respectfully with them?
Use these sentence starters to help!

- I have a great idea. We could …

- I like your idea, but what about …

- We could use both ideas because …

- Maybe we could try that, or maybe we could try …

- We can do _____ first and then _____ after that.

- This time let's use my idea, but next time I promise that we can use yours!

S.T.E.A.M. Activity

Create a Peaceful Picture in a Group

Directions: Using the materials provided, paint a picture with your group. Notice that a paintbrush is not in the list of materials. You'll have to use the other materials creatively to paint your picture!

Time Constraints: You may use a total of 30 minutes for your picture. You are allowed 10 minutes to plan and 20 minutes to paint. When you're done, discuss why your picture is peaceful.

Discussion: Did you make sure each person was able to share his or her idea? Was anybody trying to be the boss? Were you a good listener? Did you respectfully agree or disagree? What worked really well? What could you do better next time?

Suggested Materials:

- Cardboard rolls
- Construction paper
- Glue
- Paint
- Pipe cleaners
- Plastic straws
- Plastic wrap
- Tape
- Safety scissors

Glossary

agreement: (uh-GREE-ment) An agreement is a plan that everyone is willing to follow.

contribute: (kun-TRIB-yoot) To contribute is to help your team or group reach its goal.

cooperation: (koh-op-ur-AY-shun) Cooperation is working together as a team.

peaceful: (PEES-full) When people are calm instead of fighting or arguing, they are peaceful.

peers: (PEERZ) Your peers are your friends, classmates, and teammates.

respect: (rih-SPEKT) To respect is to show that you care about a person, place, thing, or idea.

To Learn More

Books

Keller, Laurie. *Do Unto Otters: A Book About Manners.* New York, NY: Square Fish Books, 2009.

Munson, Derek. *Enemy Pie.* San Francisco, CA: Chronicle Books LLC, 2000.

Sornson, Bob. *The Juice Box Bully: Empowering Kids to Stand Up for Others.* Northville, MI: Ferne Press, 2010.

Web Sites

Visit our Web site for links about respecting peers:
childsworld.com/links

Note to Parents, Teachers, and Librarians: We routinely verify our Web links to make sure they are safe and active sites. So encourage your readers to check them out!

Index

A

agreement, 12

C

compromise, 14

contribute, 16

cooperation, 12

F

fair, 10, 11, 12

P

peaceful, 15, 16, 17

peers, 16

R

respect, 8, 10

respectfully
disagreeing, 6, 17

S

sharing ideas, 5, 6, 11

T

teams, 12, 13